WILLIAMS-SONOMA

FOODMADEFAST
grilling

RECIPES

Rick Rodgers

GENERAL EDITOR

Chuck Williams

PHOTOGRAPHY

Tucker + Hossler

contents

30 MINUTES START TO FINISH

15 MINUTES HANDS-ON TIME

MAKE MORE TO STORE

about this book

When prepared on the grill, beef and pork, chicken and seafood, vegetables of all varieties, and even fruit emerge succulent and flavorful. Grilling is the ideal technique for busy home cooks, especially if you own a gas grill. It is easy to master and allows you to serve satisfying meals with minimal effort. Many of this book's recipes can can go from the kitchen to the table in less than half an hour. Others require just 15 minutes to assemble. Still others make enough to serve one night and to create quick additional meals later in the week.

You'll find such classics as smoked salmon, barbecued ribs, and whole chicken, along with recipes featuring international flavors, from Tandoori Lamb Chops and Chicken with Tuscan Herbs to Vegetable Quesadillas and Italian Burgers with Peppers & Onions. Accompany any of these main courses with a simple side dish, and you and your family can enjoy a home-cooked meal any night of the week.

Chuck

30 minutes
start to finish

herbed flank steak with tomatoes

Flank steak, 1, about 1½ lb (750 g)

Tomatoes, 2 large or 4 medium, halved crosswise and seeded

Olive oil, 2 tablespoons, plus more for brushing

Salt and freshly ground pepper

Herbes de Provence, 1 tablespoon

Fresh goat cheese, ½ cup (2 oz/60 g) crumbled

Red wine vinegar, 2 teaspoons

Mixed salad greens, 2 cups (2 oz/60 g)

SERVES 4

1 **Season the beef and tomatoes**
Prepare a gas or charcoal grill for direct grilling over high heat (see page 97 for details). If using a gas grill, turn one burner on low and the other burner(s) on high. If using a charcoal grill, spread the coals into a slope. Brush the flank steak and tomatoes all over with some oil. Season the steak with salt and pepper, and then sprinkle the herbs on both sides of the steak. Season the tomatoes with salt and pepper.

2 **Grill the beef and tomatoes**
Lightly oil the grill rack. Place the tomatoes, cut side up, over the coolest area of the grill. Place the steak over the hottest area and cover. Grill the steak, turning once, for 8–10 minutes total for medium-rare. During the last 2 minutes, sprinkle an equal amount of the goat cheese into each tomato half. Transfer the steak to a platter. Leave the tomatoes on the uncovered grill to keep warm. Let the steak stand for 3–5 minutes, then thinly slice across the grain.

3 **Prepare the salad**
Meanwhile, in a bowl, whisk together the vinegar and a pinch of salt and pepper. Slowly whisk in the 2 tablespoons oil. Add the mixed salad greens and toss until evenly coated. Transfer the tomatoes to the platter with the steak and serve with the mixed greens.

cook's tip

You may substitute crumbled blue cheese, such as Gorgonzola, for the goat cheese. Or, omit the cheese and spread the cut side of each tomato half with 1 tablespoon basil pesto or olive tapenade before grilling.

cook's tip

Olio santo (holy oil) is a tasty condiment for the steaks. To make it, in a small saucepan over low heat, combine ⅓ cup (3 fl oz/ 80 ml) olive oil; 2 cloves garlic, crushed; 2 fresh rosemary sprigs; and ½ teaspoon red pepper flakes. Heat gently for 5 minutes. Transfer to a small bowl and let cool. Spoon over the steaks at the table.

florentine t-bone with spinach

1 Cook the spinach

Prepare a gas or charcoal grill for direct grilling over high heat (see page 97 for details). In a saucepan over medium heat, warm the oil. Add the pancetta and cook, stirring occasionally, until lightly browned, about 5 minutes. Add the garlic and cook until fragrant, about 30 seconds. Stir in the spinach a handful at a time and cook just until wilted, about 5 minutes total. Season with salt and pepper. Cover the pan to keep warm.

2 Grill the steaks

Season the steaks with salt and pepper. Lightly oil the grill rack. Grill the steaks, turning once, 6–8 minutes total for medium-rare. Transfer the steaks to warm plates and the spinach to a serving bowl and serve.

Olive oil, 1 tablespoon

Pancetta or thick-cut bacon, 3 oz (90 g), chopped

Garlic, 1 clove, minced

Baby spinach, 1 ¼ lb (625 g), rinsed but not dried

Salt and freshly ground pepper

T-bone steaks, 4, each about 1 inch (2.5 cm) thick

SERVES 4

pork chops with peaches

Ancho chile powder or other chile powder, 2 teaspoons

Ground cumin, 1 teaspoon

Salt

Garlic powder, ¼ teaspoon

Bone-in, center-cut loin pork chops, 4, each about ¾ inch (2 cm) thick

Canola oil, for brushing

Peaches, 2 large firm-ripe, halved and pitted

Mango chutney, 2 tablespoons (optional)

SERVES 4

1 Prepare the grill

Prepare a gas or charcoal grill for direct grilling over high heat (see page 97 for details). If using a gas grill, turn one burner on medium-low and the other burner(s) on high. If using a charcoal grill, spread the coals into a slope.

2 Prepare the pork chops and peaches

In a small bowl, stir together the chile powder, the cumin, ¾ teaspoon salt, and the garlic powder. Brush the pork chops on both sides with oil and sprinkle with the chile mixture. Brush the peaches lightly with oil. Set aside.

3 Grill the pork chops and peaches

Lightly oil the grill rack. Place the pork chops over the hottest area. Grill until the undersides are seared with grill marks, about 2 minutes. Turn and grill about 2 minutes longer. Move the pork chops to the cooler area of the grill and cover. Grill until the chops feel firm and spring back when pressed in the center, 6–8 minutes longer. During the last 5 minutes of grilling, place the peaches, cut side down, over the hottest area of the grill and grill until the undersides are seared with grill marks, about 3 minutes. Turn and spread with the chutney, if using. Grill until heated through, about 2 minutes longer. Transfer the peaches to a cutting board and slice into thick wedges. Serve the peaches alongside the pork chops.

cook's tip

When peaches are out of season, use ½-inch (12-mm) slices of peeled and cored pineapple. Grill, turning once, until the pineapple is

slightly charred and heated through, about 8 minutes total. To peel and core a fresh pineapple, cut away the peel with a sharp knife. Slice the pineapple crosswise, then use a 1-inch (2.5 cm) round biscuit cutter to remove the core.

cook's tip

Lime butter is a fine way to
embellish corn on the cob. Grate
the zest from 1 lime into a bowl
and add ½ cup (4 oz/125 g)
room-temperature unsalted butter.
Mix well, season with salt and
freshly ground pepper, and let
stand at room temperature
for about 30 minutes before
serving to blend the flavors.

orange-chipotle chicken with corn

1 Marinate the chicken

Prepare a gas or charcoal grill for direct grilling over high heat (see page 97 for details). One at a time, place the chicken breasts between 2 sheets of plastic wrap and lightly pound with a flat meat mallet or a rolling pin to even thickness. In a shallow, nonreactive dish, combine the orange zest and juice, vinegar, oil, garlic, oregano, chile powder, and ¾ teaspoon salt. Add the chicken and turn to coat evenly. Cover and let stand while the grill heats. (The chicken can be refrigerated for up to 4 hours; turn occasionally in the marinade.)

2 Grill the corn and chicken

Lightly oil the grill rack. Place the corn on the grill and cover. Grill for 10 minutes. Add the chicken breasts with any clinging marinade to the grill. Cover and grill, turning the corn and chicken occasionally, until the corn husks are charred and the chicken is nicely browned on the outside and feels firm when pressed, about 10 minutes longer. Transfer the chicken and corn to a platter and serve.

Boneless, skinless chicken breast halves, 4, about 7 oz (220 g) each

Grated orange zest and juice, from 1 large orange

Balsamic vinegar, 2 tablespoons

Olive oil, 2 tablespoons

Garlic, 1 clove, minced

Dried oregano, 1 teaspoon

Chipotle chile powder or other chile powder, ¼ teaspoon

Salt

Corn, 4 ears, unhusked

SERVES 4

italian burgers with peppers & onions

Yellow onion, 1 large, cut into half-moons ¼ inch (6 mm) thick

Red bell pepper (capsicum), 1, seeded and cut lengthwise into strips ¼ inch (6 mm) wide

Olive oil, 2 tablespoons

Salt and freshly ground pepper

Ground (minced) beef, 1½ lb (750 g)

Pesto, 4 tablespoons (2 fl oz/60 ml), purchased

Garlic, 2 cloves, minced

Mayonnaise, ½ cup (4 fl oz/125 ml)

Round Italian rolls, 4, split horizontally

SERVES 4

1 **Prepare the ingredients for grilling**
Prepare a gas or charcoal grill for direct grilling over high heat (see page 97 for details). In a bowl, toss the onion and bell pepper with the oil to coat, then season with salt and pepper. Place the vegetables in the center of a 12-inch (30-cm) long sheet of heavy-duty aluminum foil. Fold the sheet and pleat at the top and sides to enclose the vegetables. In a bowl, combine the beef, 2 tablespoons of the pesto, the garlic, 1 teaspoon salt, and ½ teaspoon pepper and mix well. Form into 4 equal patties. In a small bowl, stir the mayonnaise and the remaining 2 tablespoons pesto together. Set aside.

2 **Grill the vegetables and burgers**
Lightly oil the grill rack. Place the vegetable packet on the grill and cover. Grill, turning occasionally, for 14 minutes. Add the patties to the grill, cover, and grill, turning once, until nicely browned on both sides, about 3 minutes on each side for medium-rare, or until done to your liking. At this point, the vegetables should be tender as well (open the packet to check). During the last minute, add the rolls, cut side down, to the grill to toast lightly. Serve the burgers on the rolls with the peppers, onions, and pesto mayonnaise.

cook's tip

Leftover grilled tuna and ginger aioli can be covered and refrigerated overnight. For a delicious sandwich, chop the tuna, add some

minced celery and fresh cilantro (fresh coriander), moisten with the aioli, and serve on toasted or grilled bread. Make an extra half recipe to ensure you have enough tuna for sandwiches the next day.

tuna steaks with ginger aioli

1 Make the aioli
Prepare a gas or charcoal grill for direct grilling over high heat (see page 97 for details). Using your hands, squeeze the juice from the shredded ginger into a small bowl and discard the ginger solids. Add the mayonnaise, garlic, and lemon zest and stir to mix. Set aside.

2 Grill the tuna
Pat the tuna steaks dry with paper towels. Lightly brush the steaks on both sides with oil, then season with salt and pepper. Lightly oil the grill rack. Place the tuna on the grill and cover. Grill, turning once, until the tuna is seared with grill marks on both sides, about 2 minutes per side for rare. Slice the steaks and serve with the aioli.

Ginger, 3 tablespoons coarsely shredded

Mayonnaise, ½ cup (4 fl oz/125 ml)

Garlic, 1 clove, minced

Grated lemon zest, from 1 lemon

Tuna steaks, 4, each about 1 inch (2.5 cm) thick

Olive oil, for brushing

Salt and freshly ground pepper

SERVES 4

snapper with green olive tapenade

Garlic, 1 clove

Pitted green olives, 1 cup
(4 oz/125 g)

Capers, 2 tablespoons, rinsed
and drained

Anchovy fillets in olive oil,
3, drained

Grated lemon zest,
from 1 lemon

Olive oil, 2 tablespoons,
plus more for brushing

Red pepper flakes,
¼ teaspoon

Snapper fillets, 4, about
5 oz (155 g) each

**Salt and freshly ground
pepper**

SERVES 4

1 Make the tapenade
Prepare a gas or charcoal grill for direct grilling over medium-high heat (see page 97 for details). If using a gas grill, turn one burner on low and the other burner(s) on high. If using a charcoal grill, spread the coals into a slope. In a food processor, chop the garlic finely. Add the olives, capers, anchovies, lemon zest, 2 tablespoons oil, and red pepper flakes and pulse until a coarse paste forms. Transfer to a bowl and set aside. Alternatively, mince the garlic, olives, capers, and anchovies with a sharp knife. Transfer to a bowl and stir in the lemon zest, oil, and red pepper flakes.

2 Grill the snapper
Pat the snapper dry with paper towels. Lightly brush the fillets on both sides with oil, then season with salt and pepper. Lightly oil the grill rack. Place the snapper over the cooler area of the grill and cover. Grill, turning once, until the snapper looks opaque when pierced with the tip of a sharp knife, about 6 minutes total. Transfer the fillets to plates, top each with a spoonful of the tapenade, and serve.

cook's tip

The grill rack must be as clean as possible to avoid the fish sticking to it. Give it an especially vigorous scrubbing with a grill brush before adding the fish. Lightly coating the fish with oil helps to discourage sticking, but don't use so much oil that it drips and causes flare-ups.

cook's tip

To make this dish vegetarian, omit the prosciutto. Or, substitute chopped grilled vegetables (page 78), warmed in a frying pan over medium heat until heated through, for the sun-dried tomatoes, then top with cheese and finish grilling.

portobellos with prosciutto & fontina

1 Prepare the garlic oil

Prepare a gas or charcoal grill for direct grilling over medium-high heat (see page 97 for details). If using a gas grill, turn one burner on low and the other burner(s) on high. If using a charcoal grill, spread the coals into a slope. In a small saucepan over low heat, combine the oil and garlic and warm gently, about 5 minutes. Remove from the heat and set aside.

2 Grill the mushrooms

Lightly oil the grill rack. Brush the mushrooms all over with the garlic oil, then place, gill side down, in the center of the grill between the hot and cool areas and cover. Grill until they give off their juices, about 3 minutes. Turn each mushroom, divide the chopped sun-dried tomatoes equally among them, and cover each with a piece of prosciutto. Cover and grill for 2 minutes. Top the mushrooms evenly with the cheese, cover, and grill until the cheese melts, about 1 minute longer. Transfer the mushrooms to plates, sprinkle with the sage, and serve.

Olive oil, 6 tablespoons (3 fl oz/90 ml)

Garlic, 4 cloves, crushed

Portobello mushrooms, 8 large, stems removed

Sun-dried tomatoes in oil, 16, drained and coarsely chopped

Prosciutto, 4 thin slices, cut in half crosswise

Fontina cheese, 6 oz (185 g), thinly sliced

Fresh sage, 2 tablespoons minced

SERVES 4

pesto shrimp on mixed greens

Grated lemon zest and juice, from 1 large lemon

Olive oil, ⅔ cup (5 fl oz/ 160 ml)

Salt and freshly ground pepper

Large shrimp (prawns), 1½ lb (750 g), peeled and deveined, tails intact

Pesto, 3 tablespoons, purchased

Mixed salad greens, ½ lb (250 g)

Grape or cherry tomatoes, 1 cup (6 oz/185 g)

SERVES 4

1 Make the lemon vinaigrette
Prepare a gas or charcoal grill for direct grilling over medium-high heat (see page 97 for details). Place a grill screen on the grill rack. In a small bowl, combine the lemon zest and juice. Gradually whisk in the oil. Season with salt and pepper. Set aside.

2 Grill the shrimp
In a bowl, toss the shrimp with 2 tablespoons of the lemon vinaigrette, ½ teaspoon pepper, and ¼ teaspoon salt. Lightly oil the grill screen. Arrange the shrimp on the grill screen and cover. Grill, turning once, until firm and opaque, about 5 minutes total. Transfer the shrimp to a bowl, add the pesto and 1 tablespoon of the lemon vinaigrette, and stir to coat the shrimp. In a large bowl, combine the greens and tomatoes, drizzle with the remaining lemon vinaigrette, and toss. Divide the salad among 4 plates, top with the shrimp, and serve.

cook's tip

Deveined shrimp are now readily available. They are easier to peel, too, since the shells are loosened in the deveining process. For

the ultimate—though more costly—time-saver, buy shrimp that are peeled and deveined. To peel and devein shrimp yourself, beginning at the head, pull off the shell, then cut a shallow groove along the curve of the back and lift out the dark, veinlike intestinal tract.

veal chops with tomato vinaigrette

1 Prepare the grill
Prepare a gas or charcoal grill for direct grilling over high heat (see page 97 for details). If using a gas grill, turn one burner on low and the other burner(s) on high. If using a charcoal grill, spread the coals into a slope.

2 Grill the veal and tomatoes
Season the veal with 1 teaspoon salt and ½ teaspoon pepper. Lightly oil the grill rack. Place the veal chops and tomatoes over the hottest area of the grill and cover. Grill the chops until the undersides are seared with grill marks, about 2 minutes. Turn and grill the other sides, about 2 minutes longer. Grill the tomatoes for the same 4-minute period, turning occasionally, until the skins are lightly charred. Transfer the tomatoes to a plate. Move the veal to the cooler area of the grill, cover, and grill for about 5 minutes longer for medium. Transfer to plates and set aside.

3 Make the tomato vinaigrette
Remove and discard the tomato skins. In a blender or food processor, combine the tomatoes and vinegar and process until puréed. With the machine running, add the oil. Then add the tarragon, ¼ teaspoon salt, and ⅛ teaspoon pepper and pulse to combine. Drizzle the veal chops with the vinaigrette and serve.

Veal rib chops, 4, each about 1 inch (2.5 cm) thick

Salt and freshly ground pepper

Plum (Roma) tomatoes, 2

Red wine vinegar, 2 tablespoons

Olive oil, ½ cup (4 fl oz/ 125 ml)

Fresh tarragon, 2 teaspoons chopped

SERVES 4

chicken kebabs with couscous

Ground cumin, 1 teaspoon

Paprika, 1 teaspoon

Ground turmeric,
1 teaspoon

Ground cinnamon,
½ teaspoon

Garlic powder, ¼ teaspoon

Cayenne pepper,
⅛ teaspoon

Salt

Boneless, skinless chicken breasts, 1¼ lb (625 g), cut into 1½-inch (4-cm) cubes

Olive oil, 2 tablespoons

Red bell pepper (capsicum), 1 large, seeded and cut into pieces

Instant couscous, 1 cup (6 oz/185 g)

Fresh cilantro (fresh coriander), 2 tablespoons chopped

SERVES 4

1 Prepare the grill
Prepare a gas or charcoal grill for direct grilling over high heat (see page 97 for details). Soak 4 bamboo skewers in water to cover while the grill heats, then drain just before using.

2 Prepare and grill the kebabs
In a small bowl, stir together the cumin, paprika, turmeric, cinnamon, garlic powder, cayenne, and 1 teaspoon salt. In a large bowl, toss the chicken with the oil to coat. Sprinkle with the spice mixture and toss again to coat. Divide the chicken and bell pepper pieces among the skewers. Lightly oil the grill rack. Place the kebabs on the grill and cover. Grill, turning occasionally, until the chicken is browned and feels firm when pressed, 8–10 minutes.

3 Make the couscous
While the chicken is grilling, in a small saucepan over high heat, combine 1½ cups (12 fl oz/375 ml) water and ½ teaspoon salt and bring to a boil. Stir in the couscous and return to a boil. Cover tightly and remove from the heat. Let stand until the couscous absorbs the water, about 5 minutes. Stir in the cilantro. Serve the kebabs with the couscous.

cook's tip

Some markets carry ready-to-grill chicken-and-vegetable skewers. Make sure they are not already marinated before you buy them, or you won't taste the Moroccan spices in this recipe. Mix together the oil and spices and then brush onto the assembled skewers.

cook's tip

Thai basil, which has purple stems, pointed leaves, and a slight anise flavor, and small Thai chiles are sold at Asian groceries and many supermarkets. If they are not available, substitute Italian basil and ½ jalapeño or serrano chile.

eggplant with spicy chile sauce

1 Prepare the grill

Prepare a gas or charcoal grill for direct grilling over high heat (see page 97 for details). If using a gas grill, turn one burner on high and the other burner(s) on low. If using a charcoal grill, spread the coals into a slope.

2 Make chile sauce

In a small frying pan over medium-high heat, warm the 1 tablespoon oil. Add the shallot, garlic, and chile and sauté until the shallot softens without browning, about 1 minute. Remove from the heat, add the fish sauce, lime juice, and brown sugar, and stir to dissolve the sugar. Set aside.

3 Grill the eggplants

Brush the eggplants with oil. Lightly oil the grill rack. Place the eggplants over the cooler area of the grill, and cover. Grill, turning occasionally, until tender, about 6 minutes. Chop the eggplants into 1-inch (2.5-cm) chunks. Spoon the rice into shallow bowls, top with the eggplant, and drizzle with the sauce. Sprinkle with the basil and serve.

Canola oil, 1 tablespoon, plus more for brushing

Shallot, 1, minced

Garlic, 2 cloves, minced

Fresh red chile, preferably Thai, 1, seeded and minced

Asian fish sauce, ⅓ cup (3 fl oz/80 ml)

Fresh lime juice, from 1 lime

Brown sugar, 1 tablespoon firmly packed

Asian eggplants (slender aubergines), 6, trimmed and halved lengthwise

Steamed rice, for serving

Fresh basil, preferably Thai, 3 tablespoons slivered

SERVES 4

salmon steaks with herbed white beans

Olive oil, 1 tablespoon, plus more for brushing

Prosciutto or bacon, 2 thin slices, chopped

Shallot, 1 large, minced

Cannellini beans, 2 cans (19 oz/590 g each), drained and rinsed

Dry white wine, 1/3 cup (3 fl oz/80 ml)

Fresh rosemary, 1 teaspoon chopped

Tomato, 1 large, seeded and diced

Salt and freshly ground pepper

Salmon steaks, 4, with skin intact

SERVES 4

1 Prepare the grill
Prepare a gas or charcoal grill for direct grilling over medium-high heat (see page 97 for details). If using a gas grill, turn one burner on high and the other burner(s) on low. If using a charcoal grill, spread the coals into a slope.

2 Prepare the white beans
In a saucepan over medium-high heat, warm the 1 tablespoon oil. Add the prosciutto and sauté until lightly browned, about 2 minutes. Add the shallot and sauté until softened, 1–2 minutes. Add the beans, wine, and rosemary and cook, stirring occasionally, until the beans are heated through and the flavors have come together, about 10 minutes. During the last 2 minutes, stir in the tomato. Season with salt and pepper. Keep warm.

3 Grill the salmon
Pat the salmon steaks dry with paper towels. Lightly brush the salmon on both sides with oil, then season with salt and pepper. Lightly oil the grill rack. Place the salmon over the hotter area of the grill. Grill, uncovered, until seared with grill marks, about 2 minutes. Turn and transfer the steaks to the cooler area of the grill, and cover. Grill until the salmon looks barely opaque when pierced in the thickest part with the tip of a sharp knife, about 7 minutes longer. Serve each salmon steak atop a portion of the beans.

cook's tip

The white bean ragout may be
made up to 2 hours ahead
and kept at room temperature.
Reheat over low heat, stirring
occasionally, just before serving.

shrimp tacos with lime slaw

1 Make the slaw

Prepare a gas or charcoal grill for direct grilling over high heat (see page 97 for details). Place a grill screen on the grill rack. In a bowl, stir together the mayonnaise and lime juice. Add the cabbage, green onions, chile, and cilantro and mix well. Season with salt and pepper. Stir in the tomato. Cover and refrigerate until serving.

2 Grill the shrimp

In a bowl, toss the shrimp with the oil, lime zest, ½ teaspoon pepper, and ¼ teaspoon salt. Lightly oil the grill screen. Arrange the shrimp on the grill screen and cover. Grill, turning once, until firm and opaque, about 4 minutes. During the last minute of grilling, add the tortillas to the grill and cook, turning once, until heated through. Transfer the shrimp to a serving bowl and the tortillas to a napkin-lined basket. Let guests make their own tacos with the shrimp, tortillas, and slaw.

Mayonnaise, ⅓ cup (3 fl oz/80 ml)

Grated lime zest and juice, from 1 large lime

Green cabbage, ½ head, cored and shredded (about 4 cups/12 oz/375 g)

Green (spring) onions, 2, white and pale green parts, chopped

Jalapeño chile, 1, seeded and minced

Fresh cilantro (fresh coriander), 2 tablespoons chopped

Salt and freshly ground pepper

Tomato, 1 large, seeded and diced

Shrimp (prawns), 1 lb (500 g), peeled and deveined

Canola oil, 1 tablespoon

Corn tortillas, 8

SERVES 4

37

tandoori
lamb chops

Garlic, 2 cloves

Yellow onion, 1 small, quartered

Ginger, 2 tablespoons chopped

Plain yogurt, 1 cup (8 oz/250 g)

Garam masala, 1 teaspoon

Salt

Cayenne pepper, ¼ teaspoon

Lamb loin chops, 4, each about 1 inch (2.5 cm) thick

SERVES 4

1 Prepare the lamb

Prepare a gas or charcoal grill for direct grilling over high heat (see page 97 for details). In a food processor, chop the garlic finely. Add the onion and ginger and pulse to chop finely. Add the yogurt, the garam masala, 1 teaspoon salt, and the cayenne and pulse to mix. Transfer to a shallow, nonreactive dish. Add the lamb and turn to coat in the yogurt mixture. Cover and let stand while the grill heats. (The lamb chops can be refrigerated up to overnight; turn occasionally in the marinade.)

2 Grill the lamb

Lightly oil the grill rack. Place the lamb chops on the grill. Grill, turning once, for 10–12 minutes total for medium-rare. Transfer to plates and serve.

cook's tip

To make an easy side dish for these Indian-inspired grilled chops, stir ½ cup (3 oz/90 g) thawed frozen peas into hot cooked basmati rice. Or, mix 2 tablespoons chopped fresh cilantro (fresh coriander) into the cooked rice.

halibut & zucchini with romesco sauce

1 Prepare the grill

Prepare a gas or charcoal grill for direct grilling over high heat (see page 97 for details). If using a gas grill, turn one burner on low and the other burner(s) on high. If using a charcoal grill, spread the coals into a slope.

2 Make the romesco sauce

Preheat a small, dry frying pan over medium heat. Add the almonds and toast, stirring almost constantly, until fragrant and golden, about 2 minutes. Pour onto a small plate. In a food processor, chop the garlic finely. Add the roasted peppers, almonds, vinegar, and paprika and process until chopped. With the machine running, pour in the 3 tablespoons oil and process to form a coarse sauce. Season with salt and pepper. Set the sauce aside at room temperature.

3 Grill the halibut and zucchini

Pat the halibut fillets dry with paper towels. Lightly brush the fillets and zucchini on both sides with oil, then season with salt and pepper. Lightly oil the grill rack. Place the halibut over the cooler area of the grill and the zucchini over the hotter area of the grill and cover. Grill the halibut and zucchini, turning once, until the halibut looks opaque when pierced with the tip of a sharp knife and the zucchini is tender, about 10 minutes. (If the zucchini is done before the halibut, move it to the coolest area of the grill.) Using a sharp knife, cut the grilled zucchini into diagonal chunks. Divide the zucchini and halibut among plates and serve with the *romesco* sauce.

Sliced (flaked) almonds, ½ cup (2 oz/60 g)

Garlic, 1 clove

Roasted red bell pepper (capsicum) strips, 1 jar (12 oz/375 g), drained (about 1 cup)

Sherry vinegar, 2 teaspoons

Paprika, preferably smoked Spanish, 1 teaspoon

Olive oil, 3 tablespoons, plus more for brushing

Salt and freshly ground pepper

Halibut fillets, 4, about 6 oz (185 g) each

Zucchini (courgettes), 4, trimmed and halved lengthwise

SERVES 4

calamari with warm potato-basil salad

Lemons, 2

Olive oil, 5 tablespoons
(3 fl oz/80 ml)

Red potatoes,
1 1/4 lb (625 g), cut into rounds
1/4 inch (6 mm) thick

Shallot, 1, minced

Fresh basil, 3 tablespoons
minced

**Salt and freshly ground
pepper**

Calamari, 1 1/4 lb (625 g)
cleaned without tentacles
(about 24)

SERVES 4

1 **Make the potato salad**
Prepare a gas or charcoal grill for direct grilling over high
heat (see page 97 for details). Grate the zest from 1 lemon
and then juice the lemon to yield 3 tablespoons. Cut the second
lemon into wedges. Set the zest, juice, and wedges aside. In
a large, nonstick frying pan over high heat, warm 2 tablespoons
of the oil until very hot. Add the potatoes and cook, stirring often,
until coated with oil and beginning to soften, about 3 minutes.
Add 1/2 cup (4 fl oz/125 ml) water, reduce the heat to medium,
and cover tightly. Cook, adding a little more water if needed
to keep the potatoes from burning, until the potatoes are tender
and the water has evaporated, about 18 minutes. Stir in the
shallot, lemon zest, and basil, and 2 tablespoons each of the
lemon juice and oil. Season with salt and pepper. Keep warm.

2 **Grill the calamari**
Using a sharp knife, slit each calamari lengthwise, then
open it flat, inside facing up. Using the tip of the knife, score
the flesh in a large crosshatch pattern. In a bowl, toss the
calamari with the remaining 1 tablespoon each lemon juice
and oil. Lightly oil the grill rack. Place the calamari on the grill
and cook uncovered, turning once, just until seared on both
sides, about 2 minutes total (it will curl). Do not overcook.
Divide the calamari and potato salad among plates and serve
with the lemon wedges.

cook's tip

Uncleaned calamari is a bargain
but is tedious to prepare, making
cleaned calamari worth the extra
expense. The tentacles are not
used here because they will fall
through the grill rack. If you want
to cook them, use a grill screen.

smoked salmon
with potato pancakes

1 Prepare the wood chips and grill

In a bowl, soak 2 large handfuls of wood chips in hot water for 10 minutes. Prepare a gas or charcoal grill for indirect grilling over high heat (see page 97 for details). For a gas grill, place a handful of dry chips on a piece of aluminum foil and set the foil on the high-heat burner. Drain the soaked chips, and when the dry chips begin to smolder, add them to the foil. For a charcoal grill, sprinkle the drained chips over the coals.

2 Smoke the salmon

Season the salmon on both sides with ½ teaspoon salt and ¼ teaspoon pepper. Lightly oil the grill rack. Place the salmon, skin side down, on the cooler area of the grill and cover. Grill until opaque when tested with a knife tip, 8–10 minutes. If the salmon is done before the pancakes, transfer to a serving platter and tent with aluminum foil to keep warm.

3 Prepare the potato pancakes

While the salmon is cooking, preheat the oven to 200°F (95°C). Line a baking sheet with paper towels and place in the oven. In a bowl, stir together the sour cream and dill; set aside. In a large bowl, mix together the potatoes, onion, whole egg, egg yolk, bread crumbs, ¾ teaspoon salt, and ¼ teaspoon pepper. In a large frying pan over medium-high heat, warm the oil until very hot. For each pancake, add about ⅛ of the potato mixture to the oil and spread into a round with the back of a spoon; do not crowd the pan. Cook, turning once, until both sides are golden brown, about 5 minutes. Transfer to the baking sheet to keep warm. Serve the salmon and pancakes with the sour cream.

Center-cut salmon fillets, 4, with skin intact, about 1 ½ lb (750 g) total weight

Salt and freshly ground pepper

Sour cream, ⅔ cup (5 oz/155 g)

Fresh dill, 2 tablespoons minced

Russet potatoes, 1 lb (500 g), peeled and shredded

Yellow onion, 1 small, coarsely shredded

Whole egg, 1

Egg yolk, 1

Fine dried bread crumbs, 2 tablespoons

Canola oil, ⅓ cup (3 fl oz/80 ml)

SERVES 4

45

15 minutes
hands-on time

bourbon-molasses chicken

Canola oil, 1 tablespoon

Yellow onion, 1 small, finely chopped

Garlic, 2 cloves, minced

Ketchup, 1 cup (8 fl oz/ 250 ml)

Molasses, ¼ cup (3 oz/ 90 g)

Balsamic vinegar, ¼ cup (2 fl oz/60 ml)

Bourbon, ¼ cup (2 fl oz/ 60 ml)

Whole chicken, 1, about 4 lb (2 kg), cut into 8 serving pieces

Salt and freshly ground pepper

SERVES 4

1 Make the bourbon-molasses sauce

Prepare a gas or charcoal grill for indirect grilling over high heat (see page 97 for details). In a heavy saucepan over medium heat, warm the oil. Add the onion and cook, stirring often, until golden brown, about 5 minutes. Stir in the garlic and cook until fragrant, about 1 minute. Stir in the ketchup, molasses, vinegar, and bourbon and bring to a boil. Reduce the heat to medium-low and simmer until slightly thickened, about 10 minutes. Remove the pan from the heat and set aside.

2 Grill the chicken

Season the chicken pieces with ¾ teaspoon salt and ½ teaspoon pepper. Lightly oil the grill rack. Place the chicken pieces, skin side down, on the rack over the drip pan, positioning the legs, thighs, and wings closest to the heat. Cover and grill, turning the pieces occasionally, until an instant-read thermometer inserted in the thickest part of a thigh or breast (but not touching bone) reads 170°F (77°C), about 50 minutes. During the last 10 minutes of grilling, brush the pieces generously with the sauce. Remove from the grill and serve.

cook's tip

This bourbon-molasses sauce is a
good all-purpose barbecue sauce.
Make a double or triple batch to
store for other meals. It will keep
in an airtight container in the
refrigerator for up to 1 month.

cook's tip

To toast sesame seeds, put them in a small, dry frying pan and place over medium heat. Toast, stirring the seeds or shaking the pan

often, until the seeds are fragrant and just beginning to turn golden brown, about 3 minutes. Keep a close eye on them, as they burn easily. Toast only the amount you need, as the seeds taste best fresh.

sesame-ginger chicken

1 Marinate the chicken
In a nonreactive bowl large enough to accommodate the chicken, whisk together the soy sauce, ginger, oil, sherry, sugar, garlic, and ½ teaspoon pepper. Add the chicken and turn to coat evenly. Cover and let stand while the grill heats. (The chicken can be refrigerated for up to 8 hours; turn occasionally in the marinade.)

2 Grill the chicken
Prepare a gas or charcoal grill for indirect grilling over high heat (see page 97 for details). Lightly oil the grill rack. Place the chicken, skin side down, on the rack over the drip pan, and cover. Grill for 25 minutes. Turn the chicken and continue to grill until an instant-read thermometer inserted in the thickest part of a thigh (but not touching bone) reads 170°F (77°C), about 20 minutes longer. Transfer to plates or a platter, sprinkle with the sesame seeds, and serve.

Soy sauce, ½ cup
(4 fl oz/125 ml)

Ginger, ¼ cup
(1 oz/30 g) shredded

Asian sesame oil,
2 tablespoons

Dry sherry, 2 tablespoons

Brown sugar,
1 tablespoon firmly packed

Garlic, 2 large cloves,
chopped

Freshly ground pepper

Whole chicken legs,
4, about 2½ lb (1.25 kg)
total weight

Sesame seeds,
2 tablespoons, toasted

SERVES 4

beer-marinated tri-tip

Lager beer, 1 cup (8 fl oz/ 250 ml)

Olive oil, 2 tablespoons

Chile powder, 1 tablespoon

Dried oregano, 2 teaspoons

Ground cumin, 1 teaspoon

Salt and freshly ground pepper

Yellow onion, 1, chopped

Garlic, 2 cloves, chopped

Tri-tip beef steaks, 2, about 1 lb (500 g) each

SERVES 6

1 Marinate the tri-tip
In a large bowl, whisk together the beer, oil, chile powder, oregano, cumin, ¾ teaspoon salt, and ½ teaspoon pepper. Stir in the onion and garlic. Add the beef and turn to coat evenly. Cover and let stand while the grill heats. (The beef can be refrigerated for up to 8 hours; turn occasionally in the marinade.)

2 Prepare the grill
Prepare a gas or charcoal grill for direct grilling over medium-high heat (see page 97 for details). If using a gas grill, turn one burner on medium and the other burner(s) on high. If using a charcoal grill, spread the coals into a slope.

3 Grill the tri-tip
Lightly oil the grill rack. Remove the beef from the marinade and place it over the hottest area of the grill. Cover and grill, turning once, for 10 minutes. Move the beef to the cooler area of the grill, cover, and grill until an instant-read thermometer inserted in the thickest part reads 130°F (54°C) for medium-rare, about 10 minutes longer. Transfer to a cutting board and let stand for 3–5 minutes, then thinly slice across the grain and serve.

cook's tip

Serve the tri-tip with grilled Yukon gold potato wedges. Parboil the potatoes in salted water for about 10 minutes, then grill alongside the beef, turning occasionally so they brown on all sides and become fork-tender.

barbecued ribs with hoisin glaze

1 Make the hoisin glaze

Prepare a gas or charcoal grill for direct grilling over medium-high heat (see page 97 for details). In a saucepan over medium-high heat, warm the oil. Add the ginger and garlic and sauté until fragrant, about 30 seconds. Add the green onion and cook until wilted, about 1 minute. Stir in the ketchup, hoisin sauce, and sherry and bring to a simmer. Reduce the heat to low and simmer, stirring often, for about 5 minutes to blend the flavors. Set aside at room temperature.

2 Grill the ribs

Cut the ribs into 4 equal portions. Season the ribs on both sides with 1½ teaspoons salt and ½ teaspoon pepper. Wrap each slab in a double thickness of heavy-duty aluminum foil. Place the foil-wrapped ribs on the grill and cover. Grill, turning the ribs occasionally and taking care not to pierce the foil, for 45 minutes. Open the foil and pierce the ribs with the tip of a knife; they should be barely tender. If not yet tender, rewrap and cook for 5–10 minutes longer. Remove the packets and unwrap the ribs, discarding the foil and juices. Add additional hot coals to the charcoal fire if the coals have burned down. Lightly oil the grill rack. Put the ribs on the grill and cook, turning occasionally, until lightly browned, about 5 minutes. Brush on both sides with the hoisin glaze and continue grilling about 5 minutes longer. Transfer to a cutting board, cut into individual ribs, and serve.

Canola oil, 1 tablespoon

Ginger, 2 tablespoons shredded

Garlic, 1 clove, minced

Green (spring) onion, 1 large, white and pale green parts, minced

Ketchup, ⅔ cup (5 fl oz/ 160 ml)

Hoisin sauce, ⅓ cup (3 fl oz/80 ml)

Dry sherry, 2 tablespoons

Baby back pork ribs, 4 lb (2 kg)

Salt and freshly ground pepper

SERVES 4–6

jerk pork tenderloin

Pork tenderloins, 2, about 1 lb (500 g) each, trimmed of silver skin

Garlic, 2 cloves

Green (spring) onions, 4, white and pale green parts, coarsely chopped

Habanero or jalapeño chile, ½, seeded

Grated lime zest and juice, from 1 lime

Soy sauce, 2 tablespoons

Canola oil, 2 tablespoons

Dried thyme, ½ teaspoon

Ground allspice, ¼ teaspoon

SERVES 6

1 Marinate the pork

If necessary, fold back and tie down the pointed "tail" of each tenderloin with kitchen string to ensure even cooking. In a food processor, chop the garlic finely. Add the green onions, chile, lime zest and juice, soy sauce, oil, thyme, and allspice and process just until a wet paste forms. Transfer to a shallow nonreactive baking dish, add the pork, and turn to coat evenly. Cover and let stand while the grill heats. (The pork can be refrigerated for up to 8 hours.)

2 Grill the pork

Prepare a gas or charcoal grill for direct grilling over high heat (see page 97 for details). Lightly oil the grill rack. Remove the pork from the marinade, place on the grill, and cover. Grill, turning occasionally, just until the pork feels firm and springs back when pressed or an instant-read thermometer reads 145°F (63°C) when inserted into the thickest part of the pork, 10–12 minutes. Be careful not to overcook the pork. Transfer to a platter and let stand for 5 minutes. Cut crosswise on the diagonal into slices ½ inch (12 mm) thick and serve.

cook's tip

Baked sweet potatoes (often
called yams) are great with the
jerk pork. Scrub medium-sized
sweet potatoes and pierce in
a few places with a fork. Place
on a baking sheet and bake in
a preheated 400°F (200°C) oven
until tender, about 1 hour.

cook's tip

You can use 1 large globe eggplant (aubergine) in place of the slender Asian eggplants, but its flesh must be salted first to draw off

some of the bitter juices. Cut crosswise into rounds ½ inch (12 mm) thick, sprinkle the rounds with salt, place in a colander, and let stand for about 30 minutes. Rinse well, pat dry, brush with oil, and grill according to the recipe.

lemongrass pork chops & eggplant

1 Marinate the pork chops
In a food processor, chop the garlic finely. Add the ginger, lemongrass, and cilantro and pulse to chop finely. Add 2 tablespoons water, the fish sauce, the brown sugar, and the red pepper flakes and process until a wet paste forms. Transfer to a shallow, nonreactive baking dish, add the pork chops, and turn to coat evenly. Cover and let stand while the grill heats. (The pork chops can be refrigerated for up to 8 hours.)

2 Grill the pork chops and eggplants
Prepare a gas or charcoal grill for direct grilling over high heat (see page 97 for details). Brush the eggplant halves on both sides with oil. Lightly oil the grill rack. Place the pork chops and eggplants on the grill and cover. Grill the chops, turning once, until they feel firm and spring back when pressed, about 8 minutes total. Grill the eggplants, turning once or twice, until tender, about 6 minutes, then move to the edge of the grill to keep warm while the pork finishes cooking. Transfer the pork chops and eggplants to a platter and serve.

Garlic, 2 cloves

Ginger, 2 tablespoons chopped

Lemongrass, 2 stalks, tough tops discarded and tender bulbs peeled and chopped

Fresh cilantro (fresh coriander), 2 tablespoons chopped

Asian fish sauce, ¼ cup (2 fl oz/60 ml)

Light brown sugar, 1 tablespoon firmly packed

Red pepper flakes, ½ teaspoon

Boneless loin pork chops, 4, each about ½ lb (250 g) and 1 inch (2.5 cm) thick

Asian eggplants (slender aubergines), 4, trimmed and halved lengthwise

Canola oil, for brushing

SERVES 4

chicken with tuscan herbs

Dried oregano, 2 teaspoons

Dried rosemary, 2 teaspoons

Dried sage, 2 teaspoons

Fennel seeds, ½ teaspoon, crushed

Salt and freshly ground pepper

Olive oil, 2 tablespoons

Garlic, 2 cloves, minced

Whole chicken legs, 4, about 2½ lb (1.25 kg) total weight

Lemon, 1 large, cut into wedges

SERVES 4

1 Season the chicken
Prepare a gas or charcoal grill for indirect grilling over high heat (see page 97 for details). In a small bowl, stir together the oregano, rosemary, sage, fennel, ½ teaspoon salt, and ½ teaspoon pepper. In a shallow, nonreactive dish, stir together the oil and garlic, add the chicken, and turn to coat evenly. Sprinkle the herb mixture evenly over the chicken. Cover and let stand while the grill heats. (The chicken can be refrigerated for up to 8 hours.)

2 Grill the chicken
Lightly oil the grill rack. Place the chicken, skin side down, on the rack over the drip pan, and cover. Grill for 25 minutes. Turn the chicken and grill until an instant-read thermometer inserted in the thickest part of a thigh (but not touching bone) reads 170°F (77°C), about 20 minutes longer. Transfer to plates or a platter and serve with the lemon wedges.

cook's tip

In the summer, when herb gardens are at their peak, substitute 1 tablespoon each finely chopped fresh oregano, rosemary, and sage for the dried herbs. Keep this same herb mixture in mind for grilling pork.

korean beef
& shiitake skewers

1 Marinate the beef

In a large, nonreactive bowl, whisk together the soy sauce, sherry, oil, green onions, pear, garlic, ginger, sugar, sesame seeds, and red pepper flakes until the sugar dissolves. Cut the beef into 1-inch (2.5-cm) cubes, add to the bowl, and mix well. Cover and let stand while the grill heats. (The beef can be refrigerated for up to 8 hours; turn occasionally in the marinade.)

2 Prepare the grill

Prepare a gas or charcoal grill for direct grilling over high heat (see page 97 for details). Soak 4 bamboo skewers in water to cover while the grill heats, then drain just before using.

3 Grill the beef skewers

Lightly oil the grill rack. Lift the beef from the marinade, and dip the mushrooms in the marinade. Thread the beef cubes and mushrooms onto each skewer. Grill the skewers, turning occasionally, for about 10 minutes total for medium-rare. Transfer to plates or a platter and serve.

Soy sauce, ⅓ cup (3 fl oz/ 80 ml)

Dry sherry, ⅓ cup (3 fl oz/80 ml)

Asian sesame oil, 1 tablespoon

Green (spring) onions, 2, white and pale green parts, finely chopped

Asian pear or Granny Smith apple, 1 small, unpeeled, cored and coarsely grated

Garlic, 2 cloves, minced

Ginger, 2 tablespoons peeled and grated

Sugar, 2 tablespoons

Sesame seeds, 1½ teaspoons

Red pepper flakes, ½ teaspoon

Beef round, 1½ lb (750 g), trimmed of excess fat

Shiitake mushrooms, about 16, stems removed

SERVES 4

pork chops with apple-sage stuffing

Unsalted butter,
2 tablespoons

Shallots, 2 tablespoons
minced

Fresh bread crumbs, 1 cup
(2 oz/60 g)

Dried apples, ½ cup
(1½ oz/45 g) coarsely
chopped

Fresh sage, 2 tablespoons
minced

Ground fennel seeds,
¼ teaspoon

Hard cider, ⅓ cup
(3 fl oz/80 ml)

**Salt and freshly ground
pepper**

**Bone-in, center-cut loin
pork chops,** 4, each about
1½ inches (4 cm) thick

Fennel bulb, 1, trimmed
and cut lengthwise into slices
¼ inch (6 mm) thick

Canola oil, for brushing

SERVES 4

1 Prepare the grill

Prepare a gas or charcoal grill for direct grilling over high heat (see page 97 for details). If using a gas grill, turn one burner on medium and the other burner(s) on high. If using a charcoal grill, spread the coals into a slope.

2 Stuff the pork chops

In a small frying pan over medium heat, melt the butter. Add the shallots and sauté until softened, about 2 minutes. Stir in the bread crumbs, dried apples, sage, and ground fennel seeds, and then mix in the cider. Season with salt and pepper. Cut a deep horizontal slit into each pork chop and fill with an equal amount of the apple stuffing. Close the slits with wooden toothpicks. Season the chops with salt and pepper.

3 Grill the pork chops and fennel

Lightly oil the grill rack. Place the pork chops over the hottest area of the grill. Grill until the undersides are seared with grill marks, about 2 minutes. Turn and grill the other sides until marked, about 2 minutes longer. Move the pork chops to the cooler area of the grill and cover. Grill until the chops feel firm and spring back when pressed in the center, about 16 minutes longer. During the last 10 minutes of grilling, brush the fennel with oil and season lightly with salt and pepper. Place over the hottest area of the grill and grill, turning occasionally, until barely tender, 8–10 minutes. Transfer the pork chops and fennel to a platter, remove the toothpicks from the chops, and serve.

cook's tip

If you don't have dried apples,
dried apricots or figs are excellent
substitutes. And if there isn't any
hard cider in the house, regular
(nonalcoholic) apple cider, dry
white wine, or dry vermouth can
be used in its place.

butterflied chicken with garlic toasts

1 Prepare the chicken and garlic

Ask your butcher to butterfly your chicken, or, to do it yourself, cut the chicken in half down one side of the backbone and breastbone, then press firmly to flatten. In a shallow, nonreactive baking dish, whisk together the wine, lemon zest and juice, 2 tablespoons oil, shallot, mustard, rosemary, ¾ teaspoon salt, and ¼ teaspoon pepper. Add the chicken and turn to coat evenly. Cover and let stand while the grill heats. (The chicken can be refrigerated for up to 8 hours; turn occasionally in the marinade.) Drizzle the remaining 1 tablespoon oil over the garlic heads and season with salt and pepper. Wrap each head in aluminum foil. Set aside.

2 Grill the chicken and garlic

Prepare a gas or charcoal grill for indirect grilling over high heat (see page 97 for details). Lightly oil the grill rack. Remove the chicken from the marinade and place, skin side down, on the rack. Place the garlic alongside the chicken. Cover and grill for 25 minutes. Turn the chicken, re-cover, and continue to grill until an instant-read thermometer inserted in the thickest part of a thigh (but not touching bone) reads 170°F (77°C) and the garlic feels tender when squeezed, about 25 minutes longer. A few minutes before the chicken is done, toast the bread over the hot area of the grill, turning once. Transfer the chicken and garlic to a carving board, let stand for 5 minutes, and then cut the chicken into quarters. Serve the chicken with the garlic heads and bread. Diners should squeeze the garlic from its papery sheaths onto the bread.

Whole chicken, 1, about 4 lb (2 kg), butterflied

Dry white wine, ½ cup (4 fl oz/125 ml)

Grated lemon zest and juice, from 1 large lemon

Olive oil, 3 tablespoons

Shallot, 1 large, chopped

Whole-grain mustard, 1½ tablespoons

Fresh rosemary, 1 tablespoon minced

Salt and freshly ground pepper

Garlic, 4 heads, top ½ inch (12 mm) cut off

Country-style bread, 4 slices

SERVES 4

make more
to store

grilled flank steak

Full-bodied red wine, 1 cup (8 fl oz/250 ml)

Soy sauce, 1/3 cup (3 fl oz/ 80 ml)

Canola oil, 1/4 cup (2 fl oz/60 ml)

Garlic, 4 cloves, coarsely chopped

Freshly ground pepper

Flank steaks, 2, about 1 1/2 lb (750 g) each

SERVES 4–6

makes 2 flank steaks total

Grill two flank steaks instead of one and you'll have an extra steak for at least two more meals. Used in sandwiches, a main-dish salad, or soft tacos, flank steak is ideal for a variety of dishes.

1 Marinate the steaks
In a shallow, nonreactive baking dish, whisk together the wine, soy sauce, oil, garlic, and 1/2 teaspoon pepper. Add the flank steaks and turn to coat evenly. Cover and let stand for 1 hour, or refrigerate, turning occasionally, for up to 8 hours.

2 Grill the steaks
Prepare a gas or charcoal grill for direct grilling over high heat (see page 97 for details). Lightly oil the grill rack. Place the steaks on the rack and cover. Grill, turning once, for 8–10 minutes total for medium-rare. The steaks should feel slightly firmer than raw meat when pressed in the thickest part. Transfer the steaks to a platter and let stand for 3–5 minutes. Thinly slice 1 steak across the grain and serve. Reserve the second steak for another meal (see Storage Tip, right).

storage tip

To store the second steak, let cool to room temperature, wrap tightly in aluminum foil or plastic wrap, and refrigerate for up to 2 days. For the most succulent and tender results, do not slice the chilled steak until ready to serve and then, using a chef's or other large, sharp knife, thinly slice across the grain at a sharp angle.

cook's tip

Horseradish mayonnaise gives
these sandwiches a spicy flavor.
It can also be used on burgers
and roast beef sandwiches or as
a dip for raw vegetables. Make
a double or triple batch and store
the extra in a tightly covered
container in the refrigerator for
up to 2 months.

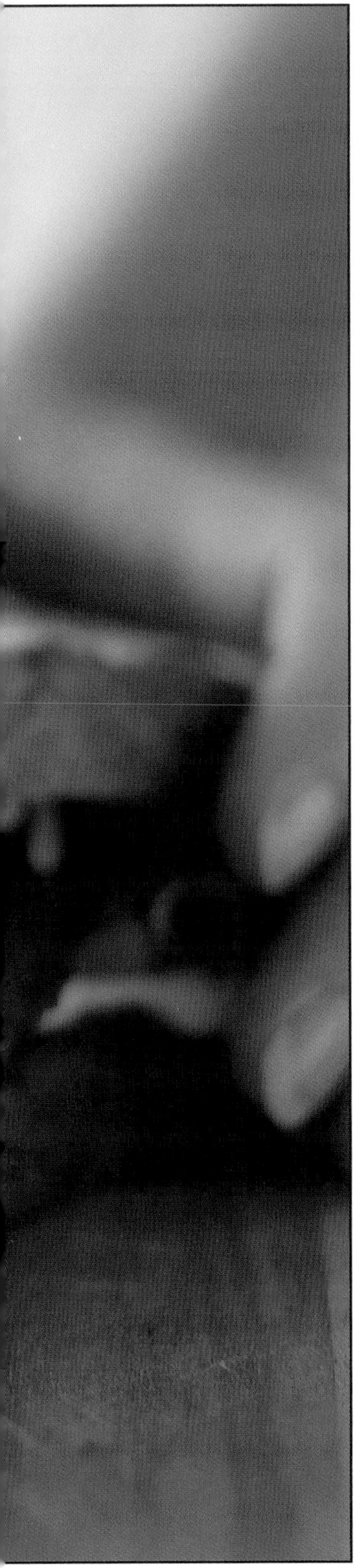

steak & tomato sandwiches

1 Make the sandwiches

In a small bowl, stir together the mayonnaise and horseradish. Thinly slice the steak across the grain. Spread the mayonnaise mixture generously on each slice of bread. Divide the steak, tomatoes, and lettuce among the slices, top with the remaining slices of bread, and serve.

Grilled Flank Steak (page 70), ½ steak

Mayonnaise, ½ cup (4 fl oz/120 ml)

Prepared horseradish, 2 tablespoons

Country-style bread, 8 slices

Tomatoes, 2, thickly sliced

Red-leaf lettuce, 4 large leaves

SERVES 4

steak, arugula &
pecorino salad

**Grilled Flank Steak
(page 70),** ½ steak

Red wine vinegar,
1½ tablespoons

Shallot, 1, minced

**Salt and freshly ground
pepper**

Olive oil, ⅓ cup (3 fl oz/
80 ml)

Arugula (rocket), 10 oz
(315 g), stems removed

Cherry or grape tomatoes,
1 lb (500 g), halved

**Pecorino romano
or Parmesan cheese,**
¼-lb (125-g) wedge

SERVES 4–6

1 **Make the shallot vinaigrette**
In a bowl, whisk together the vinegar, shallot, ½ teaspoon salt, and ¼ teaspoon pepper. Gradually whisk in the oil.

2 **Make the salad**
Thinly slice the steak across the grain. In a large bowl, combine the arugula, tomatoes, and steak. Add the vinaigrette and toss well. Using a vegetable peeler, shave curls of the pecorino over the salad. Divide among large plates and serve.

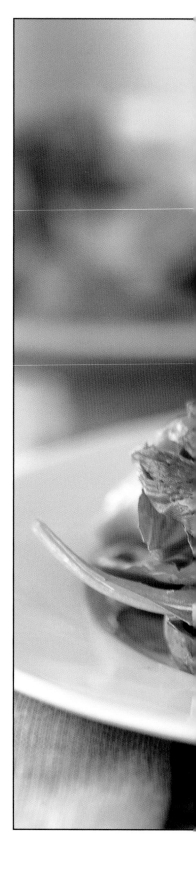

cook's tip

You can make the vinaigrette up to 5 days in advance and store it in an airtight container in the refrigerator. Shake or whisk well before using. It is a good "house dressing," too, complementing almost any mixed green salad, so make a double batch to have extra on hand.

cook's tip

When you don't have the time to make your own guacamole or salsa, you can find good-quality prepared guacamole and fresh tomato salsa in the refrigerated section of the supermarket.

steak tacos
with guacamole

1 Warm the tortillas and steak
Preheat the oven to 350°F (180°C). Stack the tortillas, wrap in aluminum foil, and place in the oven until hot, about 10 minutes. Thinly slice the steak across the grain, wrap in aluminum foil, and warm in the oven during the last 5 minutes of heating the tortillas.

2 Make the guacamole
Meanwhile, in a bowl, using a fork, mash together the avocados, salsa, and lime juice. Season with salt and pepper. Transfer to a serving bowl.

3 Serve the tacos
Unwrap the tortillas and place in a napkin-lined basket. Unwrap the steak and arrange it on a plate. Place the lettuce in a bowl. Put the steak, tortillas, guacamole, and lettuce on the table and let guests make their own tacos.

Grilled Flank Steak (page 70), ½ steak

Corn tortillas, 12

Avocados, 2, halved, pitted, and peeled

Fresh tomato salsa, 1 cup (8 fl oz/250 ml)

Fresh lime juice, from 1 lime

Salt and freshly ground pepper

Romaine (cos) lettuce, ½ small head, thinly shredded (about 2 cups/3 oz/90 g)

SERVES 4

summer
vegetable kebabs

Dry white wine, ½ cup (4 fl oz/125 ml)

Salt and freshly ground pepper

Olive oil, ¼ cup (2 fl oz/ 60 ml)

Eggplant (aubergine), 1 small, about ½ lb (250 g), trimmed and cut into chunks

Zucchini (courgettes), 2, trimmed and cut into chunks

Yellow squashes, 2, trimmed and cut into chunks

Red onion, 1, quartered lengthwise and separated into double-thick wedges

Red bell pepper (capsicum), 1, seeded and cut into large pieces

Cremini mushrooms, 16 large, trimmed

Pesto, 2 tablespoons, purchased

SERVES 4

makes 8 kebabs total

Fresh vegetables are a delicious, healthy alternative to meat on grilled kebabs. Lightly marinated and smoky from the grill, these vegetables can also be used as the foundation for subsequent meals.

1 Prepare the grill
Prepare a gas or charcoal grill for direct grilling over high heat (see page 97 for details). Soak 8 long bamboo skewers in water to cover while the grill heats, then drain just before using.

2 Prepare the vegetables
In a large bowl, whisk together the wine, ½ teaspoon salt, and ½ teaspoon pepper. Gradually whisk in the oil. Add the eggplant, zucchini, yellow squashes, onion wedges, bell pepper, and mushrooms and toss gently to coat evenly. Let stand for 5 minutes. Thread the vegetables onto the skewers, dividing the eggplant, zucchini and yellow squash, red onion, red pepper, and mushrooms evenly between the skewers. Pour any remaining marinade into a smaller bowl.

3 Grill the kebabs
Lightly oil the grill rack. Place the skewers on the grill and cover. Grill, turning as needed to cook evenly and basting occasionally with the reserved marinade, until all the vegetables are tender, 8–10 minutes. Serve 4 of the kebabs, drizzling them with the pesto. Reserve the remaining 4 kebabs for another meal (see Storage Tip, right).

storage tip

To store the vegetables, remove
them from their skewers and let
cool to room temperature, then
pack into an airtight container
and refrigerate for up to 3 days.
They do not freeze well.

cook's tip

Nearly any tube-shaped pasta,
such as ziti or penne, can be
served with this chunky, rustic
sauce. These pastas work well
because their hollows trap bits
of the vegetables, so each bite
carries both pasta and sauce.

rigatoni with goat cheese & vegetables

1 Prepare the vegetables

Bring a large pot of lightly salted water to a boil. Meanwhile, in a large frying pan over medium heat, warm the oil. Add the garlic and sauté until fragrant, about 1 minute. Add the tomatoes and cook, stirring often, until they give off their juices, about 3 minutes. Add the chopped vegetables and cook, stirring often, until heated through, about 5 minutes. Season with salt and pepper. Reduce the heat to low to keep warm.

2 Cook the pasta

Add the rigatoni to the boiling water and cook, stirring often, until al dente, about 10 minutes or according to the package instructions. Scoop out ½ cup (4 fl oz/125 ml) of the cooking water and then drain the pasta.

3 Finish the dish

Return the drained pasta to its pot. Add the vegetable mixture, goat cheese, and basil and toss well, adding a few tablespoons of the cooking water to loosen, if needed. Cook briefly over low heat to blend the flavors, then serve. Pass the Parmesan at the table.

Summer Vegetable Kebabs (page 78), 4 kebabs, vegetables removed and coarsely chopped

---

Olive oil, 3 tablespoons

Garlic, 2 cloves, minced

Cherry tomatoes, 1 lb (500 g), halved

Salt and freshly ground pepper

Rigatoni, 1 lb (500 g)

Fresh goat cheese, 1 cup (4 oz/125 g), crumbled

Fresh basil, ¼ cup (⅓ oz/ 10 g) minced

Parmesan cheese, 1 cup (4 oz/125 g) freshly grated

SERVES 4–6

81

vegetable & sausage ragout with polenta

Summer Vegetable Kebabs (page 78), 4 kebabs, vegetables removed and coarsely chopped

Olive oil, 3 tablespoons

Smoked Italian sausages, 2, sliced

Garlic, 1 clove, minced

Tomatoes, 3 large, seeded and diced

Chicken broth, ½ cup (4 fl oz/125 ml)

Salt and freshly ground pepper

Milk, 1½ cups (12 fl oz/ 375 ml)

Instant polenta, ¾ cup (5½ oz/170 g)

Unsalted butter, 3 tablespoons

Fresh sage, 2 tablespoons minced

SERVES 4

1 **Make the ragout**
In a frying pan over medium heat, warm the oil. Add the sausage slices and sauté until browned, about 3 minutes. Add the garlic and sauté until fragrant, about 1 minute. Add the tomatoes and cook, stirring often, until they give off their juices, about 3 minutes. Add the chopped vegetables and cook, stirring often, until heated through, about 5 minutes. Stir in the broth and season with salt and pepper. Reduce the heat to low to keep the ragout warm.

2 **Make the polenta**
In a saucepan over high heat, combine the milk, 1½ cups (12 fl oz/375 ml) water, and ¾ teaspoon salt and bring to a boil. Whisk in the polenta, return to a boil, and reduce the heat to low. Cook, whisking often, until the polenta is thick, about 5 minutes. Remove from the heat, cover tightly, and keep warm.

3 **Make the sage butter**
In a small saucepan over medium-low heat, melt the butter. Add the sage and cook until the butter is fragrant with the sage, about 2 minutes. Remove from the heat. Spoon the polenta into bowls and top with the ragout. Spoon the sage butter on top and serve.

cook's tip

To seed tomatoes easily and
quickly, cut them in half crosswise.
Hold each half cut side down
over a bowl and squeeze gently
to dislodge the seeds, easing
them out with a finger if needed.

cook's tip

To speed up the making of this
dish, if you have 2 large frying
pans, you can cook 4 quesadillas
at once and get supper to the
table twice as fast. Quesadillas
lend themselves to all kinds of
fillings. Experiment with leftover
shredded chicken or sliced steak,
beans, and cheeses suitable
for melting.

vegetable
quesadillas

1 Prepare the quesadillas

Spread out the tortillas evenly on a work surface. Divide the cheese and chopped vegetables evenly between the tortillas, sprinkling the bottom half of each tortilla evenly with the cheese then with the vegetables. Fold the tortilla in half to enclose the filling and press firmly. Stack the quesadillas on a plate and set aside. Preheat the oven to 200°F (95°C). Preheat a large frying pan over medium heat until hot.

2 Cook the quesadillas

Brush the pan lightly with oil. Place 2 quesadillas in the pan. Cook until the undersides are lightly toasted, about 2 minutes. Flip and toast the other sides, about 2 minutes longer. Transfer to a baking sheet and keep warm in the oven. Repeat with the remaining quesadillas, brushing the pan with oil between batches. Cut each quesadilla into wedges. Sprinkle with the cilantro and serve. Pass the salsa at the table.

Summer Vegetable Kebabs (page 78), 4 kebabs, vegetables removed and coarsely chopped

Flour tortillas, 8, about 8 inches (20 cm) in diameter

Pepper jack or Monterey jack cheese, 2 cups (8 oz/250 g) shredded

Canola oil, about 1 tablespoon

Fresh cilantro (fresh coriander), 3 tablespoons for garnish

Fresh tomato salsa, 1 cup (8 fl oz/250 ml)

SERVES 4

classic grilled whole chicken

Whole chickens, 2, about 4 lb (2 kg) each, neck and giblets removed

Olive oil, 3 tablespoons

Dried oregano, 1 tablespoon

Salt and freshly ground pepper

SERVES 4

makes 2 chickens total

Perfectly grilled chicken will have crispy skin and succulent meat. In this recipe you cook two chickens, so you can serve one tonight and store the other to use in the recipes on the following pages.

1 Prepare the chickens
Prepare a gas or charcoal grill for indirect grilling over high heat (see page 97 for details). Brush the outside of each chicken with the oil and sprinkle with the oregano. In a small bowl, stir together 1½ teaspoons salt and ¾ teaspoon pepper and season each bird inside and out with the mixture. Let stand while the grill heats.

2 Grill the chickens
Lightly oil the grill rack. Place the chickens on the rack over the drip pan and cover the grill. Grill for 45 minutes, rotating the chickens occasionally to ensure even browning. (If using a charcoal grill, add 12 more briquettes at this point to keep the fire hot.) Continue grilling until an instant-read thermometer inserted in the thickest part of a thigh (but not touching bone) reads 170°F (77°C), about 30 minutes longer. Remove from the grill and let stand for 10 minutes. Carve 1 chicken and serve. Reserve the remaining chicken for another meal (see Storage Tip, right).

storage tip

To store the whole chicken, let cool to room temperature, wrap tightly in plastic wrap, and refrigerate for up to 2 days. Or, remove the meat, discarding the skin and bones (or save them to make stock); you should have about 1 lb (about 2 cups/500 g) meat. Pack into 1 or more airtight containers and freeze for up to 3 months.

cook's tip

For another meal, make the
sandwiches with your favorite
chutney, extra-sharp Cheddar
cheese, and thinly sliced green
apple instead of the pesto,
mozzarella, and red peppers
(capsicums), and omit the
arugula (rocket). This version
is especially good on whole-
wheat (wholemeal) bread.

chicken panini with pesto & mozzarella

1 Prepare the sandwiches
Spread the pesto on the bread slices. For each sandwich, layer 2 mozzarella slices; half each of the red pepper, the chicken, and the arugula; and 2 more mozzarella slices.

2 Refrigerate the sandwiches
Spread the outside of each sandwich with half of the butter. Put the sandwiches on a sheet of waxed paper and refrigerate until the butter is firm, about 20 minutes.

3 Cook the sandwiches
Preheat a ridged frying pan or grill pan over medium heat until hot. Place the sandwiches in the pan and weight down with a second frying pan. Cook until the undersides are golden, about 2½ minutes. Turn, weight the sandwiches again, and cook until the second sides are golden, about 2½ minutes longer. Cut the sandwiches in half and serve.

Classic Grilled Whole Chicken (page 86), breast meat, cut into 6 slices (about 5 oz/155 g total weight)

Pesto, 3 tablespoons, purchased

Crusty white sandwich bread, 4 slices

Fresh mozzarella cheese, 5 oz (155 g), cut into 8 thin slices

Roasted red pepper (capsicum) in vinegar, 1 small, halved

Arugula (rocket), 6 oz (185 g), stems removed

Unsalted butter, 3 tablespoons, at room temperature

SERVES 2

chicken
cobb salad

Classic Grilled Whole Chicken (page 86), 2½ cups (1 lb/500 g) coarsely chopped meat

Bacon, 6 slices, chopped

Eggs, 2

Red wine vinegar, 2 tablespoons

Dijon mustard, 1 teaspoon

Garlic, 1 clove, minced

Salt and freshly ground pepper

Olive oil, ½ cup (4 fl oz/ 125 ml)

Mixed salad greens, about ¾ lb (375 g)

Gorgonzola or other blue cheese, ¼ lb (125 g), crumbled (1 cup)

Avocados, 2, halved, pitted, peeled, and sliced

Tomatoes, 2, seeded and chopped

SERVES 4–6

1 Cook the bacon
In a frying pan over medium-high heat, fry the bacon, stirring occasionally, until crisp and brown, about 5 minutes. Transfer to paper towels to drain and cool.

2 Boil the eggs
In a small saucepan, combine the eggs with water to cover and bring to a boil over medium heat. As soon as the water boils, remove the pan from the heat and cover. Let stand for 10 minutes. Drain the water from the pan, then run cold water over the eggs until they are cool enough to handle. Peel the eggs and slice them.

3 Make the vinaigrette
In a small bowl, whisk together the vinegar, mustard, garlic, ¼ teaspoon salt, and ¼ teaspoon pepper. Gradually whisk in the oil. In a large bowl, toss the salad greens with the vinaigrette. Arrange the chicken, Gorgonzola, avocado slices, tomatoes, bacon, and eggs on top of the greens and serve.

cook's tip

To save a little time, use a high-quality bottled vinaigrette in place of the homemade one. You may vary the salad ingredients, using sliced salami, cubed ham, or sliced smoked turkey instead of the chicken and bacon.

cook's tip

Slightly stale corn tortillas will retain their shape better than soft, fresh ones in this dish. If you have only fresh ones, let them stand uncovered at room temperature for about 8 hours. If you are pressed for time, put them directly on the oven racks for about 10 minutes while the oven preheats.

layered green enchiladas

1 Make the tomatillo sauce

Preheat the oven to 400°F (200°C). In a large frying pan over medium heat, warm 1 tablespoon of the oil. Add the onion and sauté until softened, about 5 minutes. Add the garlic and chile and sauté until the garlic is fragrant, about 1 minute. Transfer to a food processor, add the tomatillos and cilantro, and process until puréed. Return the pan to medium heat, add the remaining 1 tablespoon oil, and then add the tomatillo sauce. Bring to a boil and cook briskly until the sauce reduces slightly, about 5 minutes. Set aside.

2 Assemble the enchiladas

Lightly oil a 9-by-13-inch (23-by-33-cm) baking dish. In a nonstick frying pan over medium heat, sauté the chicken just until warm, about 3 minutes. Spoon ½ cup (4 fl oz/125 ml) of the tomatillo sauce into the dish. Line the dish with 5 of the tortillas in an even layer, tearing them as needed to fit. Sprinkle with half of the chicken and ¾ cup (3 oz/90 g) of the cheese, then spread with one-third of the remaining sauce. Repeat with 5 more tortillas, the remaining chicken, another ¾ cup of the cheese, and half of the remaining sauce. Finish with the remaining tortillas, sauce, and cheese. Pour the cream evenly on top.

3 Bake the enchiladas

Bake until the cheese melts and starts to brown, and the sauce is bubbling around the edges, about 20 minutes. Let stand for 5 minutes, then serve.

Classic Grilled Whole Chicken (page 86), 2½ cups (1 lb/500 g) coarsely chopped meat

Canola oil, 2 tablespoons

Yellow onion, 1 large, chopped

Garlic, 2 cloves, chopped

Jalapeño chile, 1, seeded and chopped

Tomatillos, 2 cans (28 oz/875 g each), drained

Fresh cilantro (fresh coriander), ¼ cup (⅓ oz/ 10 g) chopped

Corn tortillas, 15, slightly stale

Monterey jack cheese, 2 cups (8 oz/250 g) shredded

Heavy (double) cream, ½ cup (4 fl oz/125 ml)

SERVES 6

the smarter cook

The secret to making grilling a regular part of your busy life is not a question of technique but of smarter cooking. You can master the basics of readying a gas or charcoal grill with only a little practice. What you do need, however, are simple, yet inventive recipes like the ones in this book, a well-stocked pantry, and a weekly meal plan.

In these pages, you'll find strategies for managing your kitchen and putting delicious grilled food on the table any night of the week. Keep your pantry well stocked and do some extra grilling on the weekend, and you'll spend less time shopping and prepping and more time enjoying good food with your family during the week. Organization means better food with less stress—and that's what being a smarter cook is all about.

grilling basics

Grilling is an easy way to cook, and it results in wonderful flavors that are only possible when foods are exposed to the heat of an outdoor grill. Once you master a few basic techniques, you can make any recipe in this book and create great grilled dishes of your own. But before you start cooking, remember that there are more ways to grill than simply putting foods directly over a hot fire.

start the fire

Begin your meal preparation by marinating and seasoning the food (if you haven't already done so earlier in the day). Then light the grill and do the rest of your prep work while the grill is heating. Always make sure the grill grate is clean before cooking.

Gas grills must be preheated for at least 15 minutes, following the manufacturer's directions. Preheating is essential when using a gas grill or the food will not brown properly.

Charcoal grills are just as easy to use as gas grills, and they give foods an appealing smoky flavor. Follow these simple guidelines:

- **Use a chimney starter** to light coals quickly and efficiently without the need for lighter fluid, which can give foods an off flavor. Loosely pack a few sheets of crumpled newspaper in the bottom of the chimney and fill with coals. Set the chimney on the grill's fire bed rack, and light the newspaper. Watch for a few minutes to make sure the bottom coals begin to glow. After about 15 minutes, all the coals should be glowing. Wearing an oven mitt, pour out the coals in an even mound onto the fire bed. Put the grill rack in place and wait until the coals are covered with white ash, about 10 minutes.

- **Charcoal** is sold in both briquettes and lump form. Briquettes, made from pulverized lump charcoal and binders, are uniform in shape and burn with an even heat. Natural lump charcoal burns into ashes faster, so you may want to reserve it for quick-cooking foods. In both cases, allow the ashes to cool for a full day before disposal.

GRILLING TIPS

prepare in the morning On days that you plan to use the grill for dinner, check supplies and get the grill set up and ready, so you'll have less to do when it's time to cook.

clean the rack Use a wire grilling brush with a scraping tool to clean the grill rack twice: once before you begin cooking to remove any accumulated debris, and once after cooking while the rack is still hot and easier to clean. Just before putting the food on the grill, grasp a wadded-up paper towel with tongs, dip it into vegetable oil, and use it to lightly oil the grill rack.

avoid flare-ups Flare-ups, which occur when fat drips from the food onto the fire, can give food an unpleasant taste and appearance. If they occur, move food to a cooler area of the grill, and be sure the grill is tightly covered.

give it a rest Allow grilled foods to sit briefly before serving, usually about 5 minutes for meat and poultry and about 3 minutes for seafood. This gives the juices time to redistribute themselves throughout the food, producing a more evenly moist result.

SAFETY TIPS

■ Never leave a lit grill unattended.

■ Have a fire extinguisher nearby.

■ To avoid cross-contamination from raw ingredients, don't use leftover marinade as a sauce, and don't baste with it during the last 5 minutes of cooking. Instead, make extra marinade and reserve it to use for basting or as a table sauce.

■ Put grilled food on a clean platter, rather than return it to the one you used to carry it to the grill.

TOOLS AND SUPPLIES

Gather your grilling tools and supplies and keep them in a cupboard near the grill, so you never have to search for them in the heat of the moment.

basting brush

extra-long oven mitts

grill fork

grill topper (perforated rack)

instant-read thermometer

long-handled spatula with wide blade

long-handled tongs

spray bottle for dousing flare-ups

flashlight or lamp for nighttime grilling

wire brush with scraper

extra charcoal or propane

wood chips

regulate the heat

Regulate the heat by adjusting the vents to control the amount of oxygen to a charcoal fire (the more oxygen, the hotter the fire), or by turning the knobs on a gas grill. To determine the heat of your fire, hold your hand, palm down, about 4 inches (10 cm) above the fire (the point where the food will be cooking). For high heat, you should be able to keep your palm there for only 2 to 3 seconds; for medium-high heat, 5 to 6 seconds; and for a medium to low fire, 8 seconds or more.

direct-heat grilling

This is the method that most grilling cooks know best, with the food cooked directly over high heat. It works well for small items that will cook through without charring in 20 minutes or less, such as steaks and chops.

indirect-heat grilling

Large cuts of meat and whole poultry require long, relatively slow cooking by the indirect method. The heat is concentrated on one side of the grill, while a drip pan (such as a foil baking pan) is put on the other side to catch fat and juices. When the food is placed over the drip pan and the grill is closed, the food cooks from the radiated heat. Wood chips are sometimes added to the heat source to impart a smoky flavor.

the sloping method

A charcoal or gas fire burns very hot, and fighting flare-ups and scorching can be challenging. However, if the fire has two areas of heat, one hot and concentrated and one lower and dispersed, the food can be seared over the hotter area and then moved to the cooler one to finish cooking. Or, you can cook one part of the meal over the appropriate zone and grill another component over the other side. Simply spread the coals in a slope in a charcoal grill; the hottest heat will come from the higher side. For a gas grill, set one burner on high, and the other(s) on low.

build flavor

Most foods can be marinated or seasoned in the morning, so they are ready to grill at dinnertime.

- **Marinades** often contain an acidic ingredient, such as lemon juice, vinegar, or wine, that helps tenderize and add flavor to the surface of foods. Most meats and poultry should marinate for at least 15 minutes or for up to 8 hours. Most fish and shellfish should marinate for no more than 20 minutes, or they may become mushy and any acids in the marinade may "cook" them. Marinate foods in glass or ceramic vessels or resealable plastic bags, never in containers made of copper, aluminum, or iron, which can impart a metallic flavor.

- **Dry rubs** are made by mixing herbs and/or spices and patting them onto foods before grilling. For the best flavor, grind the ingredients to a fine powder in a mortar or spice grinder.

- **Pastes** combine dry seasonings with moist ingredients, such as garlic and oil. They are best made in a blender or food processor.

- **Basting sauces and glazes,** such as barbecue sauce, usually contain sugar, which caramelizes, forming an attractive sheen and adding flavor. They are brushed on foods during the last few minutes of cooking, so the sugar doesn't have time to burn. For extra flavor, use a bundle of fresh herbs, such as rosemary, as a basting brush.

- **Wood chips,** usually made from maple, alder, hickory, applewood, or mesquite, and sold with charcoal and barbecue supplies, impart a smoky flavor to grilled foods. Soak the chips in hot water for 30 minutes and then drain before using.

  FOR GAS GRILLS, place a handful of dry chips on a piece of aluminum foil set over the heat source on the high-temperature area of the grill. When the chips start to smolder, add a handful of soaked, drained chips to the foil, and additional handfuls at 45-minute intervals for long-cooked foods.

  FOR CHARCOAL GRILLS, sprinkle 3 or 4 handfuls of soaked, drained chips directly over the hot coals. Add more chips at 45-minute intervals.

WHEN IS IT DONE?

Grilled beef and lamb cooked medium-rare should feel somewhat firmer than raw meat when pressed in the thickest part. Pork and poultry should spring back when pressed. Shrimp (prawns) and many fish are done when just opaque throughout. For meat and poultry, you can use an instant-read thermometer, inserted into the thickest part of the flesh (but not touching bone), to determine doneness.

- Beef and lamb (medium-rare): 130°–140°F (54°–60°C).

- Pork (medium-rare): 145°–160°F (63°–71°C).

- Poultry (medium): 150°–160°F (65°–71°C) in breast 165°–175°F (74°–80°C) in thigh

SKEWERS

metal skewers are a good choice because they are reusable and their flat shape helps hold food in place. Make sure they are cool enough to handle before putting them on plates.

bamboo skewers are inexpensive and disposable. Soak them in warm water for about 30 minutes before using to keep the exposed ends from burning.

natural skewers, such as lemongrass stalks and rosemary sprigs (stripped of their leaves), will enhance the flavor and appearance of grilled foods.

Most of the recipes in this book can be prepared indoors if you are short on time or the weather is not right for outdoor grilling. Whichever of the following methods you choose, it is important to have adequate ventilation in your kitchen.

grill pan Designed for use on the stove top, these heavy pans have ridges that make attractive grill marks and allow fat to drain away. Many also have nonstick surfaces that make cleanup easy. Preheat grill pans over medium-high heat for several minutes before adding food.

electric grill pans With a design similar to an electric sandwich press, these countertop appliances grill both sides of the food at once. Ridged cooking surfaces make nicely seared grill marks. Some models have a variable hinge that allows you to cook foods of different thicknesses.

broiler (grill) Preheat for at least 15 minutes before using. If desired, put a cast-iron griddle in the broiler before preheating. This way, the food sears faster because it cooks on both sides simultaneously. Watch food carefully as it cooks; it can burn easily.

fireplace grill These small grates designed for cooking over embers in the fireplace are becoming increasingly popular and are a good option for wintertime indoor grilling. Many come with an adjustable grate so you can vary the distance from the fire.

make the most of your time

Grilling can be a bit more time-consuming than other cooking methods, but if you are well organized in the kitchen and at the store, you can enjoy great grilled food any time.

- **Stock up.** Over the weekend, check the pantry and refrigerator for staples you'll need during the week. When you use an item, replace it the next time you shop.

- **Shop less.** If you make a weekly meal plan, you should only need to shop two or three times a week.

- **Do it ahead.** Do as much as you can in advance. For example, make marinades, slice vegetables and meat, prepare skewers, or gather ingredients and set up the grill in the morning to save time later.

- **Double up.** Make extra for the next night. See the master recipes and second-night recipes in "Make More to Store" for ideas. Or, after the food is cooked, use the hot grill to cook vegetables for another meal.

use shortcut ingredients

When it comes to grilling, good-quality store-bought ingredients can save time and make your work in the kitchen easier. Here are a few examples:

- **Ready-made kebabs** Look for preassembled skewers of meat, poultry, or seafood in the butcher case. If they are not already seasoned, you can use your own marinade or dry rub.

- **Bottled salad dressings** Many dressings can double as marinades, basting sauces, and condiments for meat, chicken, or fish.

- **Sauces and spreads** Use premade sauces, such as tapenade, pesto, romesco, peanut sauce, and barbecue sauce, for basting during the last few minutes of grilling or as a table sauce.

- **Dry rubs and herb blends** Grilling rubs with flavors from Asian to Cajun are available in the spice section of most supermarkets. You can also use herb or other seasoning blends, such as herbes de Provence.

plan your meals

The key to smarter grilling is planning ahead. This means working out a meal plan for the week, thinking about how to fit grilling into your schedule, and stocking up on pantry, refrigerated, and frozen items (pages 104–107). With these tasks done, you can turn out satisfying grilled meals in record time, even on a busy weeknight.

During the weekend, make a meal plan for the week. This will save you hours of shopping and prep time and provide opportunities for you to grill more than you need for one meal. Depending on the season, include two or more grilled meals in your weekly plan. See the menus to the right for ideas, and look at the "Make More to Store" recipes, starting on page 70, for ways to plan two meals from a single night's grilling. Once you have worked out your menus, make a list of the ingredients you will need to supplement what is in your pantry.

- **Match your menus to your schedule.** Once you have chosen your main dishes, the next step is to decide which night to serve each one. Prepare "Make More to Store" recipes on the weekend or on an evening when you usually have extra time. For busy weeknights, choose recipes that can be almost fully prepared in advance.

- **Think about do-ahead steps.** Determine which components of each meal can be prepared ahead of time, including marinades, sauces, toppings, and side dishes. If you are grilling something that calls for a marinade, you can usually begin marinating it in the morning.

- **Think seasonally.** Choose recipes that make the most of what is in season. In-season ingredients are often less expensive, so you'll enjoy the best flavor and save money. Also, no matter where you live, you can make the recipes in this book year-round—even when the weather doesn't allow for outdoor grilling—by cooking them indoors (page 99).

- **Make the most of the grill.** On nights when you are preparing a grilled main dish, use the grill to prepare other parts of the meal, including the vegetable, an ingredient for the salad, or even grilled fruit for dessert.

THINK SEASONALLY

Using seasonal vegetables guarantees dishes with great flavors every time you cook. Use this guide to match recipes with the best each season has to offer.

spring Prepare light entrees and salads that highlight spring vegetables like asparagus, leeks, and green (spring) onions and fresh herbs, such as basil and cilantro (fresh coriander).

summer Use your grill to prepare seafood, poultry, or meats and serve with the season's abundant bell peppers (capsicums), eggplants (aubergines), cucumbers, green beans, greens (such as arugula/rocket and spinach), snow peas (mangetouts), tomatoes, and zucchini (courgettes).

autumn Include the best of the harvest in your menus with mushrooms, onions, potatoes, pumpkins, and yams.

winter Use your broiler (grill) to prepare hearty recipes using winter's bounty, including hearty greens, winter squash, and root vegetables. Incorporate the flavors of the season by using fresh herbs that are also available, such as sage and rosemary.

bruschetta Grill thick slices of country-style bread, rub with garlic, and sprinkle with olive oil, coarse salt, and freshly ground pepper. If desired, drizzle with balsamic vinegar or top with chopped tomatoes tossed with olive oil and basil.

salads A simple mixed green salad complements most grilled foods, or halve hearts of romaine (cos), brush lightly with olive oil, grill briefly, and drizzle with blue cheese dressing. You can also grill tomato halves, or grill extra vegetables one night to toss into a salad the next night.

grilled vegetables Most vegetables can be sliced; tossed with olive oil, salt, and pepper; and grilled on a grill topper, directly on the grill rack, or in an aluminum foil packet (page 18). Serve hot or at room temperature plain or drizzled with lemon juice or vinaigrette.

grilled polenta Tubes of precooked polenta can readily be found in most supermarkets. Slice the polenta ½ inch (12 mm) thick, brush lightly with olive oil, and arrange on the grill. Grill until lightly browned and the surface is crisp, about 2 minutes per side.

fruit Grill thick pineapple slices or pitted and halved, ripe but firm plums, peaches, nectarines, or mangoes, turning once, until warmed through. Serve warm or at room temperature as a side dish, or mix with diced jalapeño, salt, and pepper for a quick fruit salsa. For dessert, serve warm and top with yogurt or ice cream and crumbled amaretti cookies.

sample meals

IN MINUTES meals include easy recipes and accompaniments that rely heavily on pantry staples and go together quickly. FIT FOR COMPANY meals include ideas for stress-free entertaining.

IN MINUTES	FIT FOR COMPANY
Herbed Flank Steak with Tomatoes (page 10) Arugula (rocket) with red wine vinaigrette Orzo pasta with lemon	**Pesto Shrimp on Mixed Greens** (page 26) Cracked crab with lemon butter *Sauvignon Blanc*
Shrimp Tacos with Lime Slaw (page 37) Black beans	**Salmon Steaks with Herbed White Beans** (page 34) Grilled asaparagus with shaved Parmesan & lemon *Pinot Noir or Chardonnay*
Eggplant with Spicy Chile Sauce (page 33) Steamed jasmine rice Steamed broccoli	**Beer-Marinated Tri-Tip** (page 52) Grilled zucchini spears *Cabernet Franc or Merlot*
Halibut & Zucchini with Romesco Sauce (page 41) Oven-roasted potatoes	**Veal Chops with Tomato Vinaigrette** (page 29) Buttered egg noodles Sautéed chard with pine nuts *Chianti Classico*
Chicken with Tuscan Herbs (page 60) Grilled bruschetta with tomatoes Grilled asparagus	**Pork Chops with Apple-Sage Stuffing** (page 64) Butter lettuce with blue cheese, walnuts & pears *Zinfandel or Côtes du Rhône*
Pork Chops with Peaches (page 14) Couscous with pine nuts	

the well-stocked kitchen

Smart cooking is about having everything you need on hand, especially when your weekly meal plan includes food cooked on the grill. Get into the habit of keeping your pantry, refrigerator, and freezer well stocked and organized, and you'll have a head start on grilling any night of the week.

On the pages that follow, you'll find a guide to the essential ingredients you need to make the recipes in this book, along with tips on keeping everything fresh, properly stored, and efficiently organized. Use these lists to find out what is already in your kitchen and what needs replacing, and then organize a shopping trip to stock up. Finally, set aside a couple of hours to get your pantry in order. It will be time and effort well spent—an investment in smarter cooking that will pay off every time you cook, whether outdoors or in the kitchen.

the pantry

A pantry is typically a closet or one or more cupboards in which you store such items as dried herbs, spices, grains, pasta, and canned foods, as well as garlic, onions, potatoes, and other vegetables that don't need refrigeration. Make sure that your pantry space is relatively cool, dry, and dark. It should also be away from the heat of the stove, which can speed spoilage.

stock your pantry

- Take inventory of what is in your pantry using the Pantry Staples list.

- Remove everything from the pantry; clean the shelves and line with paper, if needed; and then resort items by type.

- Discard items that have passed their expiration date or have a stale or otherwise questionable appearance or odor.

- Make a list of items that you need to replace or stock.

- Shop for the items on your list.

- Restock the pantry, organizing items by type so things are easy to find.

- Write the purchase date on perishable items and label bulk items.

- Keep staples you use often toward the front of the pantry.

- Keep dried herbs and spices in well-sealed containers, preferably in a separate spice or herb organizer, shelf, or drawer.

keep it organized

- Look over the recipes in your weekly menu plan and check your pantry to make sure you have all the ingredients you'll need.

- Rotate items as you use them, moving the oldest ones to the front of the pantry so they will be used first.

- Keep a list of the items you use up so you can replace them.

BBQ SAUCE

Just as barbecue comes in many different guises, from the New England clambake to a smoky Texas brisket, so do barbecue sauces. They can be sweet and tangy, thick or thin, tomato or vinegar based, spicy or mild. You will also find versions with neo-Asian flavors like ginger and sesame (true Chinese barbecue sauce is very intense and should be used sparingly), and Latin brands heady with chiles. Keep your favorites on hand to slather on grilled foods to add depth of flavor with minimal effort. Refrigerate any leftover sauce until the next time you grill.

SPICE RUBS

An all-purpose spice blend is key to grilling. You can purchase a range of spice rubs in all different flavors, or you can make them yourself. When you find one you like (such as the ancho-cumin mixture on page 14, or the Tuscan herbs on page 60), make a large batch and store in a covered jar in a cool, dark place for up to 3 months.

dried herbs & spices Dried herbs and spices start losing flavor after 6 months. Ethnic markets and natural-food stores often sell spices and dried herbs in bulk. They are usually fresher and less costly than their prepackaged counterparts at supermarkets. Buy in small quantities, store them in airtight containers labeled with the purchase date, and replace often.

oils Unopened bottles of oil can be stored in a cool, dark place for 1 year, but their flavor diminishes over time. Store opened bottles at cool room temperature for 3 months or in the refrigerator for several months.

grains & pasta Store grains in airtight containers for up to 3 months. The shelf life of most dried pastas is 1 year. Although safe to eat beyond that time, they will have lost flavor. Once you break the seal on a package, transfer what you don't cook to a resealable plastic bag or other airtight container and return it to the shelf.

fresh pantry items Store in a cool, dark place and check occasionally for sprouting and spoilage. Don't store potatoes alongside onions; when placed next to each other they produce gases that hasten spoilage.

canned foods Discard cans that show signs of expansion or buckling. Also throw away cans or jars with metal lids that show evidence of rust. Once a can is opened, transfer the unused contents to an airtight container and refrigerate.

DRIED HERBS & SPICES

allspice

black peppercorns

cayenne pepper

chile powder

cinnamon

cumin

fennel seeds

garam masala

garlic powder

oregano

paprika

red pepper flakes

rosemary

sage

salt

sesame seeds

thyme

SAUCES & CONDIMENTS

Asian fish sauce

basil pesto

hoisin sauce

ketchup

mayonnaise

mustard

soy sauce

FRESH PANTRY ITEMS

garlic

potatoes

shallots

yellow onions

CANNED & JARRED FOODS

anchovy fillets

cannellini beans

capers

molasses

pitted green olives

roasted red bell peppers

(capsicums)

sun-dried tomatoes in oil

OILS & VINEGARS

Asian sesame oil

balsamic vinegar

canola oil

olive oil

red wine vinegar

PASTAS & GRAINS

instant couscous

instant polenta

long-grain white rice

rigatoni

WINE, BEER & SPIRITS

bourbon

lager beer

red wine

sherry

white wine

MISCELLANEOUS

bread crumbs

brown sugar, light & dark

corn tortillas

sliced (flaked) almonds

the refrigerator & freezer

Once you've stocked and organized your pantry, you can apply the same time-saving strategies to your refrigerator and freezer. The refrigerator is ideal for storing meats, poultry, seafood, vegetables, and leftovers. Freezing can preserve most of the flavor and nutrients in some fruits and vegetables, in most meats and poultry, and in certain leftovers. The freezer is also good for storing sauces for future use.

general tips

- Foods lose flavor under refrigeration, so proper storage and an even temperature of below 40°F (5°C) is important.

- Freeze food at 0°F (-18°C) or below to retain color, texture, and flavor.

- Don't crowd foods in the refrigerator or freezer. Air should circulate freely to keep foods evenly cooled.

- To prevent freezer burn, use only moistureproof wrappings, such as aluminum foil, airtight plastic containers, or resealable plastic bags.

leftover storage

- You can store most prepared main dishes in an airtight container in the refrigerator for up to 3 days or in the freezer for up to 3 months.

- Check the contents of the refrigerator at least once a week and discard any old or spoiled food.

- Let food cool to room temperature before refrigerating or freezing.

- Transfer the cooled food to an airtight plastic or glass container, leaving room for expansion if freezing. Or, put it in a resealable freezer bag, expelling as much air as possible before sealing.

- Freezing leftovers in small batches allows you to heat up just enough for one or two servings.

- Thaw frozen foods in the refrigerator or in the microwave. To avoid bacterial contamination, never thaw at room temperature.

KEEP IT ORGANIZED

clean first Remove items a few at a time and wipe down the refrigerator with warm, soapy water and a sponge, then rinse well with clear water. Clean your freezer at the same time.

rotate items Check the expiration dates on refrigerated items and discard any that have exceeded their time. Also toss out items that look questionable.

stock up Use the list on the opposite page as a starting point to decide which items you need to buy or replace.

shop Shop for the items on your list.

date of purchase Label items that you plan to keep for more than a few weeks, writing the date directly on the package or on a piece of masking tape.

WINE STORAGE

Once a wine bottle is uncorked, the wine is exposed to air, eventually causing it to taste like vinegar. Store opened wine in the refrigerator for up to 3 days. Use a vacuum wine pump to prolong shelf life.

meat, poultry & seafood storage

■ Most seafood should be used the same day you purchase it.

■ Use or freeze fresh meat and poultry within 2 days of purchase. If buying packaged meats or poultry, check the expiration date and use before that date.

■ Place packaged meats on a plate in the coldest part of the refrigerator. If only a portion of the meat is used, discard the original packaging and rewrap in fresh wrapping.

■ When freezing raw meat, poultry, or seafood, remove it from the original packaging and wrap in one- or two-serving portions, which can be individually thawed as needed.

fresh herb & vegetable storage

■ To store parsley, trim the stem ends, stand the bunch in a glass of water, drape a plastic bag loosely over the leaves, and refrigerate.

■ Wrap fresh herbs in a damp paper towel, slip into a plastic bag, and store in the crisper. Rinse and stem all herbs just before using.

■ Store tomatoes and eggplants (aubergines) at room temperature.

■ Cut about ½ inch (12 mm) off the end of each asparagus spear, stand the spears, tips up, in a glass of cold water, and refrigerate, changing the water daily. The asparagus will keep for up to 1 week.

■ Keep mushrooms in a paper bag (the paper absorbs excess moisture, which can cause spoilage) in the refrigerator for up to 4 days.

■ Rinse leafy greens (such as chard), spin dry in a salad spinner, wrap in damp paper towels, and store in a resealable plastic bag in the crisper for up to 1 week.

■ Store other vegetables in resealable bags in the crisper and rinse before using. Sturdy vegetables will keep for up to a week; more delicate ones will keep for only a few days.

index

Oxmoor House

OXMOOR HOUSE

Oxmoor House books are distributed by Sunset Books
80 Willow Road, Menlo Park, CA 94025
Telephone: 650 321 3600 Fax: 650 324 1532

Vice President/General Manager Rich Smeby
National Accounts Manager/Special Sales Brad Moses
Oxmoor House and Sunset Books are divisions of
Southern Progress Corporation

WILLIAMS-SONOMA
Founder & Vice-Chairman Chuck Williams

THE WILLIAMS-SONOMA FOOD MADE FAST SERIES
Conceived and produced by Weldon Owen Inc.
814 Montgomery Street, San Francisco, CA 94133
Telephone: 415 291 0100 Fax: 415 291 8841

In collaboration with Williams-Sonoma, Inc.
3250 Van Ness Avenue, San Francisco, CA 94109

Photographers Tucker + Hossler
Food Stylist Kevin Crafts
Food Stylist's Assistant Alexa Hyman
Text Writer Steve Siegelman

Library of Congress Cataloging-in-Publication data is available.
ISBN-13: 978-0-8487-3145-8
ISBN-10: 0-8487-3145-X

WELDON OWEN INC.

Chief Executive Officer John Owen
President and Chief Operating Officer Terry Newell
Chief Financial Officer Christine E. Munson
Vice President International Sales Stuart Laurence
Vice President and Creative Director Gaye Allen
Vice President and Publisher Hannah Rahill
Art Director Kyrie Forbes Panton
Senior Editor Kim Goodfriend
Editor Emily Miller
Designer and Photo Director Andrea Stephany
Associate Editor Lauren Hancock
Assistant Editor Juli Vendzules
Production Director Chris Hemesath
Color Manager Teri Bell
Production and Reprint Coordinator Todd Rechner

A WELDON OWEN PRODUCTION
Copyright © 2007 by Weldon Owen Inc. and Williams-Sonoma, Inc.
All rights reserved, including the right of reproduction in
whole or in part in any form.

Set in Formata
First printed in 2006
10 9 8 7 6 5 4 3 2 1
Color separations by Bright Arts Singapore
Printed by Tien Wah Press

Printed in Singapore

ACKNOWLEDGMENTS
Weldon Owen wishes to thank the following people for their generous support in producing this book:
Heather Belt, Ken DellaPenta, Judith Dunham, Marianne Mitten, Leigh Nöe, Sharon Silva, and Kate Washington.

A NOTE ON WEIGHTS AND MEASURES
All recipes include customary U.S. and metric measurements. Metric conversions are based on
a standard developed for these books and have been rounded off. Actual weights may vary.